The Teacher's Pocket Guide to...

By Mike Gershon

Text Copyright © 2018 Mike Gershon

All Rights Reserved

About the Author

Mike Gershon is known in the United Kingdom and beyond as an expert educationalist whose knowledge of teaching and learning is rooted in classroom practice. His online teaching tools have been viewed and downloaded more than 3.5 million times, making them some of the most popular of all time.

He is the author of over 100 books and guides covering different areas of teaching and learning. Some of Mike's bestsellers include books on assessment for learning, questioning, differentiation, growth mindsets and stretch and challenge. You can train with Mike online, from anywhere in the world, via TES Institute. He regularly delivers CPD and INSET in schools across the UK and Europe.

Find out more at www.mikegershon.com

Training and Consultancy

Mike offers a range of training and consultancy service covering all areas of teaching and learning, raising achievement and classroom practice. Examples of recent training events include:

- Using Growth Mindsets to Develop Resilient Learners

- AfL Unlocked: Practical Strategies for Classroom Success

- Stretching and Challenging More-Able Learners

- Effective Questioning: Developing a Toolkit of Strategies to Raise Achievement

- Differentiating for Whole-Class Teaching

To find out more, visit:

www.mikegershon.com

www.gershongrowthmindsets.com

Or get in touch via mike@mikegershon.com

Other Works from the Same Author

Available to buy now on Amazon:

The Teaching Assistant's Pocket Guide Series:

The Teaching Assistant's Pocket Guide to Growth Mindsets

The Teaching Assistant's Pocket Guide to Questioning

The Teaching Assistant's Pocket Guide to Feedback

The Teaching Assistant's Pocket Guide to Differentiation

The Teaching Assistant's Pocket Guide to Assessment for Learning

The Teaching Assistant's Pocket Guide to Supporting Less-Able Learners

The Teaching Assistant's Pocket Guide to Positive Behaviour Management

The Teaching Assistant's Pocket Guide to Metacognition

The Teaching Assistant's Pocket Guide to Supporting EAL Learners

The Teaching Assistant's Pocket Guide to Teaching and Learning

The 'How To...' Series:

How to use Differentiation in the Classroom: The Complete Guide

How to use Assessment for Learning in the Classroom: The Complete Guide

How to use Bloom's Taxonomy in the Classroom: The Complete Guide

How to use Questioning in the Classroom: The Complete Guide

How to Develop Growth Mindsets in the Classroom: The Complete Guide

How to use Discussion in the Classroom: The Complete Guide

How to Manage Behaviour in the Classroom: The Complete Guide

How to Teach EAL Students in the Classroom: The Complete Guide

How to use Feedback in the Classroom: The Complete Guide

How to be an Outstanding Trainee Teacher: The Complete Guide

The 'Quick 50' Series:

50 Quick Ways to Stretch and Challenge More-Able Students

50 Quick Ways to Create Independent Learners

50 Quick Ways to go from Good to Outstanding

50 Quick Ways to Support Less-Able Learners

50 Quick Ways to Get Past 'I Don't Know'

50 Quick Ways to Start Your Lesson with a Bang!

50 Quick Ways to Improve Literacy Across the Curriculum

50 Quick Ways to Improve Feedback and Marking

50 Quick and Brilliant Teaching Ideas

50 Quick and Brilliant Teaching Techniques

50 Quick and Easy Lesson Activities

50 Quick and Ways to Help Your Students Secure A and B Grades at GCSE

50 Quick and Ways to Help Your Students Think, Learn and Use Their Brains Brilliantly

50 Quick Ways to Motivate and Engage Your Students

50 Quick Ways to Outstanding Teaching

50 Quick Ways to Perfect Behaviour Management

50 Quick and Brilliant Teaching Games

50 Quick and Easy Ways Leaders Can Prepare for Ofsted

50 Quick and Easy Ways to Outstanding Group Work

50 Quick and Easy Ways to Prepare for Ofsted

50 Quick and Easy Ways to Outstanding English Teaching (with Lizi Summers)

50 Quick and Brilliant Ideas for English Teaching (with Lizi Summers)

50 Quick and Easy Ways to Build Resilience through English Teaching (with Lizi Summers)

Other Books:

More Secondary Starters and Plenaries

Secondary Starters and Plenaries: History

How to be Outstanding in the Classroom

Teach Now! History: Becoming a Great History Teacher

The Exams, Tests and Revision Pocketbook

The Growth Mindset Pocketbook (with Professor Barry Hymer)

Series Introduction

The 'Teaching Assistant's Pocket Guide' series developed out of my desire to give teaching assistants across the country a set of practical, useful books they could call on to help them in their work. Having worked with teaching assistants throughout my teaching career and knowing full well the hugely positive impact they can have on learners in a whole variety of different classrooms, I thought it was high time there was a series of books dedicated to supporting them in their working lives.

Each volume in the series focuses on a different aspect of teaching and learning. Each one aims to give teaching assistants a quick, easy way into the topic, along with a wide range of practical strategies and techniques they can use to support, guide and develop the learners with whom they work.

All of the books are designed to help teaching assistants. Each one goes out of its way to make their lives easier, and to help them develop professionally. But, crucially, the ultimate aim of each book is to give teaching assistants the tools they need to better support the learners they spend their time working with.

The whole series is written with the classroom in mind. This is a collection practical of books for what is a practical job.

I hope you find the series useful, interesting and informative. I hope it helps you to develop your work in the classroom and, of course, I hope it helps you to work ever more effectively with your learners on a daily basis.

Acknowledgements

My thanks to all the staff and students I have worked with past and present, including all the teachers and teaching assistants, particularly those at Pimlico Academy and King Edward VI School, Bury St Edmunds. Thanks also to the teachers and teaching assistants who have attended my training sessions and who always offer great insights into what works in the classroom. Finally, thanks to Kall Kwik BSE for their great design work and thanks also to the Education Endowment Foundation for their illuminating research on the role of teaching assistants.

Table of Contents

Chapter 1 – Why does feedback matter?..12

Chapter 2 – What makes good feedback?.....................................20

Chapter 3 – Giving Verbal Feedback...28

Chapter 4 – Verbal Feedback Techniques.....................................36

Chapter 5 – Scaffolding and Modelling Verbal Feedback............44

Chapter 6 – Giving Written Feedback...52

Chapter 7 – Written Feedback Techniques....................................61

Chapter 8 – Scaffolding and Modelling Written Feedback...........69

Chapter 9 – Feedback Troubleshooting 77

Chapter 10 – Conclusion: Recapping and Next Steps 85

Select Bibliography 92

Chapter 1 – Why does feedback matter?

Research suggests time and again that feedback is one of the most effective strategies we can use to raise student achievement. For more on this, see John Hattie's *Visible Learning* (Routledge, 2008) and the Education Endowment Foundation's Teaching and Learning Toolkit (educationendowmentfoundation.org.uk).

Feedback matters because it helps learners. It gives them information they can use to improve their work, to make changes, and to adapt what they are doing. Feedback is one of the most important ways through which learners develop an understanding of what success looks like and what they need to do to be successful.

To illustrate this point, let us imagine two different classrooms.

In Classroom One, all learners receive feedback. This comes from the teacher and the teaching assistant. It is a mixture of verbal and written feedback, delivered by both through the course of the year.

In Classroom Two, no learner receives any feedback. Neither the teacher nor the teaching assistant give feedback. There is no written feedback and no verbal feedback.

Take a moment to think about the different experiences learners would have in each classroom. Imagine you had to choose one of the classrooms for yourself, or for your own children. Which one would you choose?

Clearly, Classroom One is the classroom we would all want to be in. The one that is undoubtedly better for the learners who are learning there.

But why is this the case? The research tells us that feedback is effective. And we can intuitively grasp this by comparing our two imaginary classrooms – one in which feedback is central and one in which it doesn't exist. But why does feedback matter? How does it work?

A Few Ideas About Feedback

I'll offer a few ideas, to help answer these questions. This should make it clearer why feedback matters. And why it has such an impact on student achievement.

In any classroom, we have two groups of people – the learner and the adults. The learners are there to learn and the adults are there to make that learning happen. The teacher plans and teaches the lesson and the teaching assistant supports them in doing this. The teacher has responsibility for the whole class, the teaching assistant may have responsibility for one learner, a selection of learners, or they may be responsible for helping out across the board.

In short, the teacher and the teaching assistant are in the classroom to help the learners learn as much as possible.

So far, so obvious.

In what ways do the teacher and teaching assistant achieve this?

We can divide the process into three – planning, teaching and assessing.

The teacher plans the lesson. They identify what they want their learners to learn and then plan how they are going to make this happen. In the ideal scenario, the teaching assistant is privy to this information. They may contribute to the planning process. At the very least, the teacher should inform them about what is going to happen so they can plan how they will support the learning and, if appropriate, specific learners who they work with.

Next comes the teaching. This is where the teacher delivers the lesson, supported by the teaching assistant. This is the most important phase. During the teaching, an environment is created in which learners are focussing on the particular things the teacher wants them to learn about. This period is suffused with interactions – between the teacher and their learners, between the teaching assistant and their learners, and between learners.

Finally, we have assessment. This takes place in two stages. First, there is the assessment which takes place during the teaching phase. This assessment is sometimes formal, but more often informal. It includes all the opportunities the teacher and the teaching assistant have to observe what learners are doing, and assess whether they are on the right track, how successful they are being and so forth.

The second assessment stage takes place after the lesson. This is usually done by the teacher, but not always. This is nearly always formal and involves the teacher marking learners' work.

Let's take a step back and think about this from a more general perspective.

A lesson is planned then delivered. During the delivery stage, assessment begins. It continues after the lesson and the results are used to inform the next stage – the planning of another lesson.

Plan, deliver, assess. Plan, deliver, assess.

This is the cycle of teaching.

By assessing what learners are doing and how they are coping with the learning, we find ourselves in a position to plan future lessons that more closely match learner needs.

The same principle applies for teaching assistants. Here, we plan how we are going to support our learners, deliver that support during the lesson, assess how learners are working in response, and then tweak and adapt our efforts so they are more in line with where learners are at. After the lesson, we reflect on what happened, assessing the interactions which took place, and think ahead to how we will further tweak and adapt things next time round.

And here we get to feedback.

Whenever we asses where learners are at, what they know, what they understand, or how they are getting on with the work, we are then in a position to offer them feedback.

We elicit information about student learning, then give feedback based on the information we elicit.

To put it another way, **we diagnose where our learners are at, then give them information they can use to understand how they are doing and to improve things.**

This means that when we give feedback, we are giving learners access to our expertise. Access to knowledge and understanding they don't yet possess. We are helping them to go beyond what they can currently do by sharing information with them. Through this process, we help shape their efforts.

And it's as simple as that.

Let me sum up the key points, then I'll illustrate these with an example.

Key Points

- Teaching consists of three things: planning, teaching and assessing.

- Teaching assistants are heavily involved the second and third of these.

- When learning is taking place, we observe what learners are doing. We read their work, listen to them, ask questions, watch what they are doing and how they do it.

- This means we are eliciting information about student learning. We are eliciting information about what learners know, understand and can do. We make an informal assessment about where learners are at.

- Armed with this information, we give learners feedback.

- Our feedback is tied to the information we have elicited.

- We assess where learners are currently at – what they know, what they understand and what they can do. Then, we give them feedback which helps them to do more, go further, or target their efforts more effectively.

- Feedback gives access to expertise – the teacher's expertise, or the teaching assistant's expertise.

- Learners can use feedback to change what they are doing, to improve, develop and grow.

Illustrative Example

In a literacy lesson, a teaching assistant is working one-to-one with a learner. The teaching assistant regularly works with this learner. They have a good relationship. The learner struggles with literacy. They find the work difficult and tend to need extra support. The teaching assistant has a good understanding of where the learner is at, what they know and what they can do. This understanding comes from working with the learner over an extended period. The teaching assistant has been able to watch the learner work, listen to them, ask them questions, read their work and so on. They have elicited lots of information about the learner's knowledge, skills and understanding.

During literacy lessons, the teaching assistant wants to support the learner, but they also want the learner to be as independent as possible. They encourage and support the learner to try things out, to work hard and to put as much effort as possible into having a go.

The teaching assistant views their main role as giving feedback. They observe what their learner does, and they then give feedback in response. For example, the learner has a go at writing a poem. The teaching assistant reads the poem, and makes a suggestion as to how the learner could improve it. The two of them talk about this, discussing the feedback. Then, when the learner is happy they understand what the feedback means, they have a go at implementing it.

They use the information the teaching assistant has provided to improve their work. To make changes they would have struggled to have made on their own, without this support.

The teaching assistant bases their feedback on the poem the learner has written, as well as their wider knowledge about the learner. They give access to their expertise. After all, they are more expert than the learner when it comes to literacy. That is why they are in the classroom, supporting the learner.

Summary

In the example we see the process of giving feedback in action. The teaching assistant uses feedback to help the learner develop their work. The interaction between the learner and the teaching assistant is underpinned by the latter's superior expertise. They give access to this expertise through their feedback. This helps the learner to learn more than would otherwise be the case. The teaching assistant's feedback enhances and develops learning. It adds something extra, taking the learner beyond what they can achieve on their own.

In the rest of this book we'll look at practical strategies and techniques you can use to make sure your feedback is of the highest standard. To make sure it supports student learning as much as possible. And to ensure it helps learners gain access to your expertise – so they can do more and learn more than would otherwise be the case.

Chapter 2 – What makes good feedback?

We'll start by looking at what makes good feedback.

There are a number of things to consider, and we'll examine each one in turn. First up is personalisation, followed by precision and relevance. Third is combining positives and negatives. Fourth is clarity and, finally, we have concision.

Personalisation

Learners are more likely to take your feedback on board if it is personalised. By this we mean two things. First, that it is personalised in terms of what learners are doing, what they have done and what they need to do next. Second, that the learner knows it is meant for them.

We can achieve the first aspect by making sure we elicit information about student learning and then use this information to inform our feedback. Our learners don't want to hear general feedback that could apply to anyone. They want to hear feedback which feels personal to them. Feedback which is closely tied to who they are and where they are at with their learning.

The second aspect can also be easily achieved. When giving feedback, use the learners name so that they know the feedback is meant for them. The aim here is to make a connection in the learner's mind between the feedback you are giving them and their sense of self. So, for example, you might start your feedback by saying something like: 'Angelica, what I've been thinking about...' or 'Hanif, why don't we try...' In both cases, personalisation is immediately signalled through the use of the learner's name.

These are fairly obvious points. But it is easy to forget them if you are working with a number of learners through the course of a lesson. Getting into the habit of using learner names as part of your feedback, and tying your feedback to what learners have done and are currently doing means you consistently personalise that feedback and so bind learners into it. This makes it more likely they will view your feedback positively, believe it is relevant to them and, ultimately, act on it.

Precision and Relevance

Which leads us nicely onto the ideas of precision and relevance.

Feedback which is imprecise or irrelevant will be viewed with scepticism by many learners. They will not feel it is for them and may come to view your feedback in a negative light if they believe it is consistently imprecise, irrelevant or both.

Consider yourself in the position of learner. If someone gave you feedback which was vague or ambiguous, how would you feel? And what if they gave you feedback you felt was irrelevant? That you felt did not connect to what you were trying to achieve?

When giving feedback it is important you ask yourself two questions:

- Is this feedback precise?

- Is this feedback relevant?

When asking the first question, consider whether the learner will be able to use your feedback as it is, without having to analyse it in any great detail. Precise feedback is feedback which relates to specific areas of student learning and which learners can use to make specific changes. Vague feedback does not possess these qualities. To illustrate, consider the differences between these two pieces of feedback:

1) I want you to improve your story. Make it better, please.

2) I want you to improve the ending of your story. Make sure it builds up and keeps the reader excited and interested right up until the end.

The first piece of feedback is imprecise. It leaves the learner with a lot to do. In some cases, this might be OK. They might be able to fathom what the teaching assistant means. But it many cases, it will leave the learner floundering. The uncertainty makes it hard for them to put the feedback to good use.

The second piece of feedback is precise. It diagnoses the problem and indicates what the learner needs to do to fix this. It doesn't do all the work for the learner, but it does show them where they need to target their effort. The feedback is easy to follow and easy to use.

Relevance usually follows on from precision, in that precise feedback is usually relevant feedback as well. But only if the precision is a result of you focussing on what the learner needs to do to improve their work now, in the present.

You can emphasise the relevance of your feedback by drawing learners' attention to what it means, why you have given it and how it relates to what they are doing. Explaining your feedback in this way helps learners quickly grasp why it is relevant to them. This makes it more likely they will see it in a positive light and make good use of it.

Positives and Negatives

Combining positives and negatives in your feedback is nearly always a good approach. Generally speaking, you should aim to provide two or three positive comments to balance out a constructive comment. For example:

'Flora, I really like the way you kept going when the learning got tough. I could see you were trying to find a solution by testing different ideas. That was a thoughtful approach to take. Next time, I'd like you to use the instruction sheet when you get stuck. It's there to help you and it takes you through the problem-solving process step-by-step. See if you can use it next time to get past any difficulties.'

In this feedback, the teaching assistant has begun by identifying what Flora has done well. This serves two purposes. First, it helps Flora develop a better understanding of what good looks like. When we identify strengths and give learners positive feedback, we help them to appreciate how we judge what is good work or good learning. In this example, the teaching assistant is helping Flora to understand that persistence, embracing challenges and using trial and error are all characteristics of good learning; things Flora should keep using in the future.

Second, it makes it easier for many learners to take on board the constructive comment. Hearing positives first predisposes learners to think more positively about any critical comments you give. While some learners will happily accept any constructive feedback, many need a bit of positive affirmation first. You might like to think about the positive comments balancing the constructive comment. When the balanced is achieved, the learner is better placed to take both types of comment for what they are – information about their learning which they can use to help themselves improve.

Clarity

Clear feedback is feedback which learners can easily assimilate and use. Feedback which is unclear, garbled or confusing is difficult to act on. It also diminishes your status as an expert who is there to support learners in their learning and to help them do more than they can do on their own.

A good tip is to think about your feedback before speaking it to your learner. This need only take a couple of seconds. Say the feedback through in your mind first. This helps you to clarify what you want to say, gives you a chance to rehearse it, and lets you order your thoughts prior to articulating them.

If you play your feedback through in your mind before delivering it, that means what learners hear is your second or third attempt at articulating your view of their learning. This will nearly always be a clearer, more accurate verbalisation of what you think. The process of running through it first in your mind is a process of refinement. The feedback you verbally deliver is thus an end product rather than a work-in-progress.

The more comfortable you get with delivering feedback, the less necessary this process becomes. At the same time, the more comfortable you get, the more quickly you'll be able to run through the process in your mind.

The same points are true of written feedback. Think about what you want to say before writing it down. Keep to short sentences and use examples to illustrate key points. All of this helps keep written feedback as clear as possible.

And remember that clarity of feedback promotes ease of understanding as well as ease of use.

Concision

The final point to consider when it comes to giving good feedback is concision. Being concise means being brief and succinct. It doesn't mean saying as little as possible. But it does mean saying as much as is necessary.

One of the risks attached to feedback is that we give learners too much information. Lengthy or overlong feedback is distracting, harder to make sense of and harder to put to use. Succinct, concise feedback takes learners swiftly to the heart of the matter. It focuses their attention and gives them something specific they can use to target their efforts.

If learners receive feedback that is lengthy or overlong, they may find their working memory overloaded. Working memory is limited to roughly seven pieces of information, plus or minus two. If we give learners reams and reams of feedback, they will quickly come up against this limit. The common response when faced with information overload is to withdraw – or to give up.

For example, try to only give learners one target at a time to focus on. While there might be many things they could improve in their work, providing a big list of these is likely to be counterproductive. On the other hand, picking out one important area for improvement and asking learners to focus all their energies on this nearly always brings about good results.

Summary

When giving feedback, think about what you are saying, what impact it will have and how easy it is for learners to make use of the information.

Good feedback tends to follow these rules:

1) It is personalised. The learner knows it is for them and feels that it addresses their current situation.

2) It is precise and relevant. The learner can see how the feedback connects to what they are doing.

3) It combines positives and negatives. The learner receives information about what they are doing well and what they can do to improve.

4) It is clear. The learner can understand it and use it.

5) It is concise. The learner is not overloaded by the feedback. They can use it to target their efforts.

Chapter 3 – Giving Verbal Feedback

Verbal feedback forms a key part of the interactions we have with learners. We give feedback on their learning which helps them to adapt and modify what they are doing. Our feedback is designed to support them. By using our feedback, they can do more than would otherwise be the case. With these thoughts in mind, here are five strategies you can use to give good verbal feedback:

Observe Then Feedback

Observe what a learner is doing, then give feedback. For example, you might be working one-to-one with a learner during a geography lesson. They set off on the task the teacher has set and you observe them as they work. After a little bit of time has passed, you step in and offer them some feedback. The learner is then in a position to change what they are doing.

This is the most common way in which we deliver verbal feedback. While obvious, there are a couple of deeper points we need to draw out.

First, observing means more than just watching learners as they work. It means thinking critically about what learners are doing as they are doing it. We need to ask ourselves questions such as: 'What are they finding easy and what are they finding difficult?' 'Are they interacting with the task in the way the teacher intended?' 'What could I say that would help them to go beyond what they are currently doing?' If we don't take a critical approach to our observation, it is less likely that the feedback will give will be useful and relevant.

Second, during the observation period, we need to assess what type of feedback is going to be must useful to the learner. To put it another way, how do we want them to target their efforts? Do we want them to focus on knowledge, on understanding, or on skills? Or is there something else we need them to think about?

What we're getting at here is that the observation process is an active one. The teaching assistant is actively engaged in assessing what the learner is doing, how they are doing it and what else they could be doing. This then leads to effective and relevant feedback being delivered in response.

Observe, Feedback, Leave, Return

A development of the previous method involves the teaching assistant observing what the learner is doing, giving feedback based on what they have observed, leaving the learner to implement the feedback, and then returning a little later to assess the extent to which the learner has acted on the feedback. For example, a teaching assistant may say something like this:

'Arthur, I really like the way you've started using the keywords in your writing. This shows you were listening to Miss Smith and you know the keywords are important. I'd now like you to try giving examples of some of the keywords. This will show you understand them really well.

I'm going to go and work with some other learners – but I'll be back in five minutes to see how you're getting on.'

This approach brings a few benefits. First, it gives the learner a chance to work independently to implement your feedback. Promoting independence is always a good thing and this technique encourages the learner to take ownership of the feedback they receive. Second, it sets a rough time limit in which the learner must act. In the example, the teaching assistant is returning in five minutes. The learner therefore knows they must target their effort now. A sense of urgency is created, emphasising the fact that the learner needs to use the feedback immediately, rather than waiting for some later point.

Third, and finally, this approach relieves a bit of the pressure some learners can feel upon receiving feedback. Sometimes, learners can find it uncomfortable if they feel they are being watched while trying to implement the feedback they've been given. By leaving and then returning, you remove this from the equation. Learners can thus work uninhibited – and can show you the end results of their efforts without feeling you are watching the development of these from start to finish.

Feedback in the Form of a Question

Not all feedback needs to be in the form of a statement. You can also deliver feedback in the form of a question. This is a subtler way of delivering feedback because it does not explicitly state what learners need to do.

Instead, it directs learners, asking them to think in a certain way. Here are three examples:

- How else could you have finished the story?

- What other methods could we try to solve the equation?

- Is that the best approach to take, or do you think another approach might be more useful?

In each of these examples, the teaching assistant is prompting their learner to think again. The feedback is subtle. It is implicit rather than explicit.

In the first example, the teaching assistant implies to the learner that there are different ways in which stories can be finished. By using this question, they encourage the learner to look again at the story they have written and to explore different options for concluding a narrative.

In the second example, the teaching assistant implies that other methods are available for solving equations. This directs the learner to think about what these different approaches might be. Through this thinking, the learner is likely to come up with different ideas for how they could try to find an answer.

In the third example, the teaching assistant implies to the learner that more than one approach is possible. This directs the learner to think critically about the approach they have used and to think through the other options which are open to them.

The examples show different ways teaching assistants can use questions to deliver feedback. In each case, what students should do next is implied, rather than explicitly stated. Learners are expected to take the lead and be independent. And, if they struggle to do this, the teaching assistant can offer further support to make things clearer.

Suggesting Alternatives

When delivering verbal feedback, you might like to suggest alternatives to your learners. This is another way of delivering feedback, one which promotes independence and encourages learners to take the lead. Here's an example:

Teaching Assistant: 'This is a really interesting sketch you've done for your poster. I think you're nearly ready to start doing the final version. Before you do, though, why don't we have a think about the title. Do you think making it bigger and more central could be a good alternative? Or, maybe the title could be in the middle of the poster? One more thing to think about is whether the title could look good if it was at the bottom of the poster, with everything growing up from it. What do you think?'

This feedback is intended to help the learner think more critically about their initial design. By suggesting alternatives, the teaching assistant is implying that different paths could be taken. This, in turn, encourages the learner to question whether or not their initial ideas are as sound as they first assumed. At the end of the questioning process they may decide to stick with their initial idea. Or, they may opt to modify their approach.

By suggesting alternatives, the teaching assistant helps the learner to think more critically and to refine their work. They also encourage the learner to be independent and to take the lead. This is because the teaching assistant is not saying what changes the learner should make but is instead offering food for thought. It is then up to the learner whether or not they take this on and use it or decide to continue on their initial path.

Drawing Attention to Strengths

In all the preceding examples we have focussed on constructive feedback. Feedback which either tells learners what they should do to improve or sends their thinking in a direction intended to spark an improvement. Our final technique is slightly different.

Drawing attention to strengths means using your feedback to highlight what learners are doing well. This is something we sometimes overlook. We want to help our learners to get better, so we often focus our feedback on what they need to do to improve. However, learners also benefit from feedback about what they are doing well.

Drawing attention to strengths serves a few purposes. First, it helps build learner confidence. If learners are unsure about whether or not they are on the right lines, feedback which draws attention to strengths can be really helpful.

Second, learners can develop their understanding of what good work looks like if they are given feedback focussing on what they are doing well. For example, a learner in a numeracy lesson who receives feedback drawing attention to their strengths will, through this process, develop a clearer sense of what they are meant to be doing in numeracy lessons – and what behaviours to repeat in the future.

Third, if learners know what their strengths are (and don't forget that many learners don't necessarily know this) then they are better equipped to target their efforts in this direction in the future. For example, our learner from the numeracy lesson will be in a position to apply themselves in a more effective manner in future numeracy lessons, as a result of having strengths-based feedback from their teaching assistant.

Summary

When giving verbal feedback, there are lots of options open to us. We should aim to follow the rules for good feedback outlined in Chapter Two. As well as this, we can think about specific strategies through which to shape our feedback. These include:

1) Critically observing what learners are doing, then giving feedback.

2) Critically observing what learners are doing, giving feedback in response, then leaving and returning a little later to see how learners have used the feedback.

3) Providing feedback in the form of a question – or a series of questions.

4) Suggesting alternatives and then discussing these with our learners.

5) Drawing attention to a learner's strengths, so as to reinforce these.

Chapter 4 – Verbal Feedback Techniques

In this chapter we continue to focus on verbal feedback. We do this by looking at five further techniques you can use when working with learners. You can use these techniques when working one-to-one with learners or when working with a small group.

Provide Two Options

Consider this example:

Teaching Assistant: 'OK, Mo, I'm going to suggest two different targets you could try working on next. You decide which one you want to go for. The first target is this: Choose one part of your book report and rewrite it using more examples from the book. The examples will help develop your points. The second target is this: Read through your book report and identify five describing words you could change for more interesting ones. Which would you like to tackle?'

This piece of verbal feedback does a couple of interesting things. It provides the learner with a choice and, in so doing, a sense of agency and control. At the same time, it lets the learner know two different ways they could improve their work, giving them a couple of things to think about in the future, the next time they write a book report.

In our example, we might imagine Mo thinking carefully about the two options the teaching assistant has provided. This means he is engaged with the feedback and assessing what has been said. This active engagement with the feedback is provoked through the provision of two options. Mo must make a choice. To make a good choice he must weigh up the alternatives. In doing this, he is also encouraged to think critically about his work – what he has produced and how it could be improved.

For all these reasons, providing two options is a useful technique to have on hand.

You can develop it further by explaining to your learners what you are doing and why. For example, our teaching assistant might say something like this:

'I want you to think carefully about your work, Mo, and I want you to be independent and in control of your learning. So, instead of telling you what to do next, I'm going to give you two options and let you decide which is best. We can discuss your thinking and see where it takes you.'

Link Your Feedback to a Positive Change

Some learners find it hard to accept feedback. Some struggle to believe that it can have a positive impact. And some find it nigh on impossible to imagine positive changes in the future, based on the implementation of your feedback. To help learners who find themselves in this situation, you can try linking your feedback to a positive change. Here's an example:

Teaching Assistant: 'Tia, what I'd like you to try now is coming up with a new design that uses all the different things we've thought about but presents them in a much clearer way. Let's call this your second draft. It's going to be a big improvement on the first draft because you've already practised once, tried your ideas out and learned from them. Now you'll be able to create an improved design that really does justice to your thinking.'

Notice how the teaching assistant connects their feedback to a positive change. They are making an explicit connection between the learner implementing the feedback and positive changes coming about as a result. This helps the learner see the feedback in a more positive light. The teaching assistant is making a prediction about the future which the learner, for whatever reason, finds it hard to make.

Delivering feedback in this way means summoning up the image of a successful future scenario – one in which the learner has used your feedback to make positive changes and therefore achieved what they were trying to do. Using this technique consistently means you can help your learners change their attitude to feedback. Over time, they will come to see the positive connection as the norm and, hopefully, be able to make it themselves without having to rely on you to do it.

Feedback on Misconceptions

When learners make misconceptions, this is a great opportunity for us to help them change their thinking. If we identify a misconception we also identify a chance to give useful, relevant feedback. Without this feedback, learners may continue labouring under the same misconceptions. And, as a result, they may continue making the same mistakes they are currently making.

If you hear or see a learner using a misconception in their work, step in and offer verbal feedback to teach away from that misconception. Make the learner aware of what you are doing. Draw their attention to the misconception and then indicate how your feedback can help them avoid it in the future.

For example, you might be working with a small group of learners during a numeracy lesson. The topic is fractions. You notice that two of the learners in your group both have a misconception around how to add fractions. They are adding the numerators and the denominators. So, for example, they think that one third plus one third is two sixths, instead of two thirds. This is a great opportunity to step in and deliver feedback to these learners, helping them to understand the misconception and how to avoid it in the future.

When you have this technique as part of your toolkit, you can actively search for misconceptions during lessons. When working with individual learners or small groups, listen carefully to what they say and closely analyse what they do. Keep your eyes and ears open, ready to pick up any misconceptions that come to the surface. On spotting one, step in and use your feedback to teach away from it.

The best thing about this technique is that it primes you to spot and remove misconceptions early on. This makes it less likely that learners will make additional mistakes further down the line. If the misconception is removed, then learners won't unwittingly return to it later.

Create a Crib Sheet

Sometimes it can be difficult to come up with good feedback on the spot. During lessons a lot happens. There is much which can draw our attention away from what we are doing. Our focus is often divided and, when it is, we cannot always guarantee our feedback will be of the highest standard.

If you find yourself in this situation, a good option is to create a crib sheet you can use to come up with verbal feedback on the spot. It works as follows.

Outside of lessons, take a sheet of plain A4 paper and write the word 'Feedback' at the centre. Draw a circle round it. Next, think of all the different areas you could give feedback on. Write each of these around the edge, then connect them to the feedback circle using a line. For example, you might include:

- Effort

- Misconceptions

- Mistakes

- Thinking

- Spelling and grammar

- Accuracy

- Creativity

When you've filled up your sheet, take a moment to look at everything you've written down. Then, decide which you believe are the most important areas you can give feedback on. Grab a different coloured pen and highlight these. This gives you a core list of categories. The categories you believe are the most crucial ones when it comes to feedback.

Use these categories to create a crib sheet. Write them up on a flashcard in a bullet point list. You might like to include a little image next to each one to help you to memorise them.

You can carry this crib sheet with you when you are in lessons. If you find yourself stuck when about to give verbal feedback, take a quick glance at the list and pick the category which feels most appropriate for the learner with whom you are working. You can give them a piece of verbal feedback based on this category and feel confident that this is relevant, useful and of a high standard.

Ask Learners What They Would Like Feedback On

Here's a completely different technique. One which turns the feedback process on its head. Usually when we give verbal feedback, we assess the work learners are doing and give them some information in response. We decide what our feedback should focus on. We base our decision on the assessment we make of students' learning.

But why not turn things around and pose one of these questions to your learners:

- What would you like me to give feedback on?

- If you had to choose one thing for me to give feedback on, what would it be?

- Can you tell me what you think I should give you feedback on? Why did you pick that area?

Each of these questions puts the onus on the learner. They all ask learners to be independent and to take control of their learning. To provide an answer to any of the questions, learners will have to think carefully about their work, weigh up different options, and come to a conclusion. They will then have to explain and justify their decision to you. Only then will they get some feedback they can use to improve things – to further develop their work and their learning.

When first introducing this technique, you need to think carefully about where your learners are at. Some will be confident enough to take it and run with it. They won't need any further help. They'll simply relish the prospect of being in control and deciding what they want your feedback to focus on.

Less confident learners might find the approach a bit trickier, initially at least. In these situations, you can try the following steps:

i) Explain to your learner why you are asking them to identify what they want feedback on.

ii) Walk them through how to analyse their own work and how to pick out an area for feedback.

iii) If necessary, give them a set of three areas to choose from. This does a bit of the work for them, helping them get to grips with the approach if they are finding it particularly difficult.

Summary

In this chapter we've examined a further five techniques you can use to give good verbal feedback. These are:

1) Providing two options from which the learner can select.

2) Linking your feedback to positive changes in the future.

3) Giving feedback on misconceptions.

4) Creating a feedback crib sheet to help you out during lessons.

5) Inviting learners to tell you the area or areas on which they would like feedback.

Chapter 5 – Scaffolding and Modelling Verbal Feedback

If learners find our feedback hard to access, we can use scaffolding and modelling to make things a bit easier for them. Scaffolding is anything we do which helps learners to access our feedback. This is where we make things a little simpler, explain things a bit more clearly or do a bit of the work for the learner. They can use the scaffold to access the feedback. It acts as a bridge or a ladder, helping them get from where they are to where we want them to be.

Modelling is where we demonstrate to learners what we want them to do with our feedback. It sees us showing learners how to use our feedback and what success looks like. They can then copy, imitate or borrow from our models. We show them what success looks like and they can then recreate that themselves.

Here are five techniques you can use to scaffold and model verbal feedback for your learners:

Break Your Feedback Down

Here is an example:

Teaching Assistant: 'I really like the way you've looked carefully at what happened to the plant when we left it in the cupboard. I can see you've been thinking like a scientist and paying attention to small details. What I'd like you to try next is writing up your findings in the same level of detail as you used when you were talking to me about them.'

Learner: 'Um, I'm not really sure...I don't know how to do that.'

Teaching Assistant: 'OK, let's break it down and see if we can do one thing at a time. First, I'd like you to make a list of all the things you noticed about the plant. Then, I'd like you to put the list in order from most to least important. Decide what you think matters the most and what matters the least. Then, I'd like you to turn your list into four paragraphs. The first paragraph should explain the most important things you noticed.'

Learner: 'OK, that helps. So, I should start with a list. OK, here goes...'

In this example, the teaching assistant responds to the learner's difficulty by scaffolding the feedback for them. They take what they originally said and break it down into a series of three steps. This makes it easier for the learner to engage with the feedback. Instead of having to work out what to do, they can follow the steps. Working through these one by one ensures they successfully implement the target the teaching assistant has suggested.

You can use this technique any time a learner struggles to make sense of your feedback. You can even take things one step further by writing down the steps. The learner then has them close to hand and can refer to them as they are working.

Can you explain it back to me?

This is a great question to ask if you are unsure whether a learner has understood your feedback. If they can explain it back to you, then brilliant, they can go off and try to put the feedback into practice. If they struggle to explain it back to you, then that is also good – because you now know this and can do something about it.

Let us concentrate on the second case, the learner who struggles to explain your feedback back to you.

In this situation, there are at least three different routes you can take to scaffold the feedback further, so that your learner is able to come to terms with it and put it to use:

1) Explain the feedback a second time, then invite the learner to explain it back to you. Listen to their explanation and then ask them questions about it. Develop a discussion with them about the feedback. Ask them why they think you have given it, how they think it might help them, and what difficulties they think they might have putting it into practice.

2) Write the feedback down and ask the learner to underline any parts of it they don't understand. As soon as the feedback is written down it becomes something the two of you can annotate, point at and refer back to. You can use this as a discussion point and a tool through which to analyse your learner's understanding of the feedback.

3) Walk your learner through what your feedback means in the context of their work. Show them how they could put it into action and explain why this would be beneficial. As you go through this process, draw your learner's attention to the fact that the feedback is about doing something different from what they are currently doing. Making this distinction helps the learner appreciate the change you are trying to effect through your feedback.

Specify What Success Looks Like

If a learner knows what success looks like then it becomes easier for them to interpret and make sense of your feedback. For example, you might be supporting a learner in an art lesson. You give them some feedback on the drawing they are doing, and then you point to a drawing on the wall of the art classroom exemplifying what you are talking about. Suddenly, the learner has a point of reference they can use to make sense of your feedback. They can say to themselves 'Ah, so that means I need to make my drawing more like the one I can see on the wall.' Or, 'Ah-ha, so what I need to do is borrow some of the techniques I can see in that drawing, because that will make my drawing look better.'

When specifying what success looks like, remember to indicate to your learner that the feedback you are giving them is intended to make their work better. Explain that you believe they can achieve the success by implementing your feedback. This way you are both helping them to understand what success looks like and making it clear that you firmly believe they can achieve that level of success.

This technique scaffolds learners' interactions with your feedback by making it easier for them to understand what your feedback means and what it is likely to lead to when implemented.

If there isn't an existing piece of work nearby to use as a reference point (as in the art example above), you can talk learners through what success will look like, show them by giving an example yourself, or list three success criteria they need to fulfil to successfully implement your feedback.

Show How to Use Your Feedback

Consider this:

Teaching Assistant: 'Laura, I'd like you to practice including one example in every paragraph you write. This will make your writing more persuasive. I'm going to show you how you can do it. I'll talk you through what I'm thinking about as I write my paragraph, then you can have a go afterwards.'

In this example, the teaching assistant gives their learner some feedback and then explains they will demonstrate how to use that feedback before asking the learner to have a go. This is modelling. The teaching assistant is modelling how to implement the feedback.

Let's think about what might happen next. The teaching assistant starts to write a paragraph while Laura watches and listens. The teaching assistant talks through their thinking. They give access to their expertise – to their understanding of how to write a paragraph and how to make sure you include an example to illustrate your points. When the teaching assistant gets to the point at which they start writing out their example, they might stop and highlight to Laura that this is happening next. This draws extra attention to it and places it at the forefront of her mind.

Working in this way means giving your learner a clear, unambiguous view of how to implement your feedback. Providing a model they can use means taking them a long way towards successful implementation of your feedback. We don't want to do all the work for our learners. But if they are really struggling to get to grips with our feedback, then explicitly showing them how to use it is a powerful technique on which we can call.

Draw Out a Plan of Action

This technique is similar to the steps method we mentioned at the start of the chapter. However, it is sufficiently different to warrant a separate entry. It works as follows.

Give your learner some feedback you want them to make use of. Talk to them about the feedback. Discuss it with them and get a sense of how well they understand it. Then, take a sheet of plain paper and draw a path on it, from one end to the other. Label the start of the path, the end of the path and three points in between. You can call those points 'A' 'B' and 'C'.

Explain to your learner that they are currently at the start of the path and that when they have successfully implemented your feedback they will be at the end of it. Indicate that points 'A' 'B' and 'C' are markers on the road to success.

At this point, you have two options open to you. First, you can invite your learner to suggest what the three markers might represent. Ask them what they think the first, second and third things they'll need to do are if they want to successfully implement your feedback. Second, you can specify what the three markers are yourself. Which option you go for will depend on how your learner feels about the feedback.

Once the path is labelled, you and your learner have a plan of action. They can use this model as a reference point for putting your feedback into practice. First they need to get to Point A, then to Point B and, finally, to Point C. This provides a nice visual reference the learner can use to check their own progress and to make sense of what they are trying to achieve and where they are trying to get to.

Summary

In this chapter we've looked at scaffolding and modelling verbal feedback. This is where we help learners to access our feedback. Scaffolding sees us doing a little bit of the work for our learners. We simplify things for them. Modelling sees us create a model learners can use to make sense of our feedback. They can borrow from the model, copy it or imitate it. The five techniques we explored are:

1) Breaking feedback down so it is easier for learners to understand.

2) Asking learners if they can explain your feedback back to you – and making changes in response to this.

3) Specifying what success looks like so learners know what they are aiming for.

4) Demonstrating how to use your feedback.

5) Drawing out a plan of action learners can use to direct their efforts.

Chapter 6 – Giving Written Feedback

Written feedback differs from verbal feedback while also retaining some similarities. The most striking similarity is that it serves the same purpose and is expressed in the same form. The purpose is to help learners improve, grow and develop. The form is a statement or question from teacher or teaching assistant to learner.

The most striking difference between written and verbal feedback is that written feedback is fixed in time and space whereas verbal feedback disappears once it has been spoken. Other differences exist, and we will explore some of them, as well as the most striking one, in this chapter.

Fixing Feedback in Time and Space

When we write something down it becomes fixed in time and space. Consider a shopping list. You can go to the shops with your thoughts of what to buy or you can go to the shops with those thoughts written on a piece of paper. When doing the latter, you take account of your capacity to forget or to lose track of what you need to buy. This is not because your memory is particularly poor, but because it is limited, like everybody else's. As soon as we turn to writing we take control of memory, overcoming its limitations.

In the same instance, we take control of time.

Consider a law that was written in, say 1915, and which remains on the statute book today. That law continues to exert its effect despite over a hundred years having elapsed since it was fixed in time and space by being written down. Similarly, when you write a shopping list, you take account of the fact that your future self will be able to use that shopping list at some unspecified point in the future. You do this without thinking about it because it is common sense to assume that writing persists into the future. Indeed, that is one of the main reasons we use it.

It is worth bearing these thoughts in mind as we turn our attention back to feedback. As soon as we write feedback down we make use of these characteristics of writing. The expansion of memory, the overcoming of memory's limitations, the persistence of writing into the future, the knowledge that it can be used by our future selves.

This is all hugely beneficial – for us and for our learners. For example:

- Once feedback is written down, learners can return to it whenever they want.

- If a learner forgets their feedback, they can turn to the page or piece of paper on which it was written and remind themselves of what it was.

- If the teacher or teaching assistant forgets what feedback they've given, they can follow the same approach.

- If feedback is written down, learners can look at it, read it, analyse it and reflect on it. Their working memory is freed up to do this more easily because they do not need to devote space to storing the feedback.

- Learners can check their work against their written feedback, to see if they've implemented it correctly.

None of this is to denigrate verbal feedback – far from it. The point is to draw attention to some of the benefits of written feedback, as well as its unique character. Points worth remembering as we move on.

When can you give the best feedback?

If you are giving verbal feedback, the answer to this question is 'at almost any time during a lesson.' Why? Because the feedback is informal, easy for learners to assimilate, directly related to what they are doing now, in the moment, and closely tied to your interactions with them during the lesson.

With written feedback, things are a little different. Written feedback takes a bit longer than verbal feedback – to write and to assimilate. It also tends to come in response to a specific piece of work. In the normal run of things, a learner completes some work, this is marked by a teacher or teaching assistant, written feedback is provided, and the learner is then given time to read this, think about it, make sense of it and, finally, apply it.

When thinking about written feedback, we therefore need to consider what will happen to it after we've given it. Or, to put it another way: How much time will learners have to think about, reflect on and apply the feedback?

If the answer to this is 'not much' then we need to think again.

For written feedback to be effective, it needs to be followed by time during which the learner can engage with it. Without this, the written feedback may get lost, disappear or be ignored.

When giving written feedback – either during a lesson or when marking a learner's work outside of lessons – ask yourself what will happen when they get that written feedback. If you think they won't have enough time to engage with it, then either find another way to deliver the feedback, or make time in which engaging with the feedback is the top priority. This way, you ensure that learners have the opportunity they need to use any written feedback you give.

Tracking Written Feedback

It can be helpful to track written feedback. This means you and your learner can see what sort of written feedback they are receiving over time. The two of you can then ask questions like:

- Is the written feedback having an impact?

- Can we see evidence of the written feedback being put into practice?

- Do we need to go back and look again at some of the feedback which has been given?

The easiest way to track written feedback is to collate it somewhere. For example, you might get a small notebook and use this. If you are working with a learner one-to-one, you might record any written feedback they receive from you and their teacher in this notebook. The two of you then have a reference point you can use to keep track of written feedback over time.

Another option is to stick a sheet in the front of learners' books in which you record their written feedback. An A4 piece of paper with three columns is suitable for this. Label the first column 'Date', the second column 'Feedback', and the third column 'How did you use the feedback?'

Periodically, you and your learner can return to this sheet to assess what feedback has been given and how that feedback has been used. If you find that your learner is not using their feedback, or is consistently receiving the same feedback, then you can talk to them about this.

One final point to note is that tracking written feedback over time is an excellent way to help your learners appreciate the progress they are making. For example, you might invite them to look at the sheet in the front of their books at the end of a three-month period. They will be able to see how their learning has developed over this time by looking at the feedback they've received and the things they've done to make use of that feedback. This can be really motivational for learners. It also helps them to understand the power of feedback and why acting on feedback is so important.

Helping Learners Feel in Control of Written Feedback

Some learners can be put off by written feedback. As we've noted, it's more formal than verbal feedback and, if learners don't feel comfortable receiving it, they might be tempted to ignore it or withdraw from it altogether. These gestures are often defensive. The kind of responses we see if learners feel like they are in danger of getting things wrong, of making mistakes or being shown up. That they feel this way is neither a reflection on us or them. But it is important we remember that their perceptions are open to change and that our approach to written feedback can help to change them.

You can help learners feel in control of written feedback in lots of ways. These include:

- By inviting them to underline anything they don't understand and then discussing these elements with them.

- By asking them to first pick out the strengths or positive features mentioned in the feedback. This draws the learner's attention to what they have done well. You can discuss these positive aspects with them before asking them to identify their target and how they think they could implement this.

- By asking learners how they think the feedback could benefit them in the future. If they struggle to answer – or don't want to answer – propose a set of options from which the learner must choose. You could even include some deliberately absurd options to bring in an element of fun.

- By comparing the written feedback the learner has received to written feedback you received at some point in the past. You can use this comparison to illustrate how you made use of your written feedback before encouraging your learner to take control in the same way.

- By challenging your learner to rewrite their feedback in the form of a simple cartoon strip. This gives the learner a way to engage with the feedback at the same time as it encourages them to synthesise it and turn it into something new. This helps them to analyse, understand and remember the feedback.

Combining Written and Verbal Feedback

Combining written and verbal feedback can be effective. When doing this, you can gain the benefits of both, giving your learners a great chance of being successful. Here are three examples of how you can do it:

1) Having provided a learner with some verbal feedback, ask them if they would like to write it down so they can remember it and use it later. If they say 'yes', ask them: 'What might the feedback look like if it was written down?' This question is designed to help the learner think about how they will capture the verbal feedback in writing. It focuses the learner's attention on the differences between the written and the spoken word. It helps them to think about how they will take what you have said – your verbal feedback – and turn it into a piece of writing which is fixed in time and space.

2) If a learner receives a piece of verbal feedback but seems to be struggling to make sense of it, ask them if they would like you to turn it into a piece of verbal feedback. If they say 'yes' read through the feedback and then offer a verbal version. This could see you reading the written version aloud or, more likely, it could involve you offering a verbal summary that is easier for the learner to access. This approach sees you using verbal feedback as a scaffold to help learners access and understand written feedback.

3) This approach is a bit different and can be a good way of engaging learners who are reluctant to use written feedback. Imagine the learner you are working with receives a piece of written feedback. They are reluctant to engage with it and so push their book away, showing this reluctance. You say, 'Let's make this written feedback into something we can listen to.' Ask the learner to get out their smartphone and then invite them to record themselves speaking the written feedback aloud. Explain that they now have a recording they can use as an alternative to the written feedback. This gives learners a completely different way of engaging with the written feedback they receive.

Summary

In starting to think about written feedback we've explored some of its key characteristics and features. We've thought about these in the context of learning and looked at the impact written feedback might have on our learners. Five things to think about, use and employ when working with learners are:

1) Remember that written feedback fixes information in time and space. This brings many benefits we and our learners can take advantage of.

2) The best time to give written feedback is when you know learners will have a chance to think about it, reflect on it and use it after they've received it.

3) You can track written feedback – something you can't do with verbal feedback.

4) There are a range of strategies you can employ to help learners feel in control of their written feedback.

5) Combining written and verbal feedback can have a good impact on student learning.

Chapter 7 – Written Feedback Techniques

When giving written feedback there are various techniques you can use to structure what you write and to help learners access and engage with the content of your writing. Here we look at five of these.

Three Strengths and a Target

This is one of the most common structures for written feedback. We begin by identifying three things the learner has done well and we follow this up with a target – something they can try to improve next time. Here is an example:

'John, I really like the way you've thought carefully about what kind of pictures you want to include in your leaflet. The front page is eye-catching and makes you want to find out more. The second page has a good mixture of writing and pictures. I'd like you to look again at pages 3 and 4. You can develop these by including more detail in your writing, so the reader gets a clear sense of what your leaflet is about.

We might imagine that John is a learner who regularly works with the same teaching assistant in his lessons. That teaching assistant gives John feedback on his work. The feedback is often verbal and sometimes written. In this instance, the teaching assistant has used 'three strengths and a target' to structure their written feedback.

In the example, we see the teaching assistant has identified three good things about John's leaflet – the thought which has gone into the picture selection, the design of the front page, and the combination of writing and images on the second page. They have then suggested how John could improve his work – by looking again at pages three and four.

By the time John gets to his target, he has had a chance to think about what he has done well. The first part of the feedback has highlighted this, motivating him to engage with the target and helping him to establish a clear idea of what good work should entail. It is arguably easier for John to take the target on board once he has already heard some of the positive messages about his work. Do note, however, that those messages are a form of feedback in themselves – this is not indiscriminate praise, but focussed, specific, relevant identification of what John has done well.

Two Stars and a Wish

Another common structure for written feedback, particularly at primary level, is two stars and a wish. This follows the same principle as 'three strengths and a target.' The learner first learns what they have done well, before finding out what they could do to improve. Two stars and a wish is nice language to use with younger learners. It often helps to engage them with feedback and can take some of the perceived sting out of the process of receiving feedback (learners may perceive a target in a more positive light if it is called a wish).

Here is an example of written feedback in the form of two stars and a wish:

Two Stars: Your recipe is creative – you've put together ingredients I've not thought of combining before. I also like your attention to detail. The drawing you've done of how the dish should look is careful, precise and clear.

One Wish: I'd like you to try the recipe out, see how it tastes and then refine it. I'm not sure two teaspoons of nutmeg is the right amount. Have a go and see what you think.

This example comes from a food technology lesson. We might imagine that a teaching assistant with a background in cooking and catering is working in a school, attached to the food technology department. In lessons, they support the teacher by working with small groups of learners, helping them to access the learning and develop their work.

In this example, the teaching assistant has given written feedback identifying two things the learner has done well and describes these as two stars. This helps the learner understand what they are doing well and what they should keep doing in the future. The target is described as a wish. This gives it a subtly different sense in the learner's mind. They may be happier to engage with a wish and to see this in a positive light as they move forward.

Red Box to Write In

How do we know that our learners have made good use of our feedback? One option is to draw a red box directly after your written feedback and to challenge your learners to redo some of their work inside this box, making use of your feedback as they do. Here's an example:

'Sonia, I'd like you to look back through the sums. 17 out of 20 are correct. In those, you've successfully applied the rules for multiplying fractions. I'd like you to identify the 3 sums you got wrong. When you've found them, have another go at them. Remember to use the rules for multiplying fractions and to think carefully about each step. Show your working in the red box so I can see it and check whether you've got your corrections right.'

In this example, we find ourselves in a numeracy lesson. The teaching assistant is working with a small group of learners. They need extra support with their maths and the teaching assistant is providing that. Sonia has finished before her peers and so the teaching assistant has marked her work to check whether it is right. They have given Sonia feedback and then drawn a red box underneath it, in which she can make her corrections.

There are two brief points to note here. First, you will see that the teaching assistant is encouraging Sonia to be proactive and independent. She needs to go back through her work and find the sums she's got wrong. Second, the red box becomes an area in Sonia's book in which she can apply her feedback and make corrections. The teaching assistant can then quickly see how Sonia has done, if she has been successful and whether she needs further support.

Give an Example

If you feel one of your learners is going to struggle with your written feedback, include an example illustrating what you are trying to communicate to them. Doing this both contextualises the feedback and provides a concrete model the learner can use as a reference point for acting on it.

Here is an example:

'Maria, I am impressed at your storyboard. I like the way you have taken the story of Little Red Riding Hood and thought about how you could transfer it to a modern-day setting. Your choice of a city is interesting. It gives you lots of opportunities to do unusual and exciting things. To improve your storyboard, I'd like you to think about how you are going to show Red Riding Hood's feelings to the audience. For example, you might have a scene in which she talks to herself about how she is feeling. Or, you might have a scene in which she posts a message on her phone explaining what she's feeling while she's at her granny's house.'

This piece of feedback follows similar rules to those outlined above. It starts with positives and then gives the learner one piece of constructive criticism on which to focus. One target to put into practice. Notice, however, that the target is illustrated through two examples. The teaching assistant has done this because they believe Maria might struggle to act on the feedback on her own. The examples give her a starting point. They are models she can borrow from or imitate. It might be that Maria decides to directly copy one of the examples. Or, she might use them as a starting point and come up with her own ideas. Either way, the examples help ensure she engages with the feedback.

Supplement with Verbal Explanation

If a learner is struggling to make sense of their written feedback, supplement it with verbal explanation. This gives the learner two opportunities to assimilate their feedback – first by reading what has been written and second by listening to what is being said.

You can use this technique when you have given a learner written feedback and you can also use it when a learner has received written feedback from the teacher. Let's look at each situation in turn.

Imagine you are working one-to-one with a learner. At the end of the lesson you take their book away and mark it. You give the learner some written feedback, return their book to them at the start of the next lesson and invite them to read through what you've written. When they've finished reading you talk them through the feedback, explaining why you've given it, what it means, and how they could use it to develop their work. Immediately, the learner is in a stronger position. Your verbal feedback has helped them to check their understanding. It has supplemented what they've understood from reading your written feedback.

We'll now move to a different scenario. It is the start of the lesson and the teacher is returning student books. You are working one-to-one with a learner who is a little behind their peers and needs some extra support. The learner receives their book, opens it up and reads through their written feedback. At the same time, you read the feedback as well. After all, this is the first time you've seen it. When the learner has finished reading, you can offer them a verbal explanation of the feedback. This explanation helps them access the meaning of what the teacher has written. It supports them in accessing the content of the feedback and, in turn, makes it easier for them to apply this in their future work.

Summary

In this chapter we've further explored written feedback, looking at a variety of techniques you can use to structure it and to help learners access, understand and engage with the written feedback they receive. The five techniques we looked at are:

1) Giving three strengths followed by a target, to help learners feel positive about constructive criticism.

2) Giving two stars and wish, achieving the same result, but in a slightly different way.

3) Drawing a red box underneath your feedback and inviting learners to show within that box how they could implement their feedback.

4) Giving examples which illustrate how learners can put your written targets into practice.

5) Supplementing written feedback with verbal explanation so it is easier for learners to make sense of the former.

Chapter 8 – Scaffolding and Modelling Written Feedback

Scaffolding and modelling written feedback is similar to scaffolding and modelling verbal feedback. In both cases we want to help learners access the feedback they've received. In both cases we want to help them make sense of their feedback – so they can implement it in their future work. Here are five techniques you can use to do this:

Breaking Down Written Feedback

Breaking down written feedback makes it easier to assimilate. Instead of having to read through all the feedback and make sense of everything at once, the learner can focus on one thing at a time. This means they can focus their attention on different aspects of the feedback and it stops them feeling overwhelmed – which they may do if they are struggling to interpret all the feedback in one go.

For example, we might have a learner who has received written feedback from their teacher. They take one look at it, decide that it is too much to deal with and so push their book to one side. At this point, the teaching assistant steps in to offer support. They take the learner's book and read through the feedback the teacher has given.

Next, they take a pen or pencil and use this to divide the written feedback in three. They label the three sections '1' '2' and '3'. Then, they invite the learner to take another look at the feedback. But, they say, start off by only focussing on the bit marked '1'. When the learner is happy they have understood this part of the feedback they can move onto the part labelled '2'. And so on.

This scaffolding technique helps learners see that feedback is usually a collection of linked statements. Dividing the feedback up means they can focus on one statement at a time. This is easier than trying to make sense of everything at once. You can even teach this technique to your learners so they can use it themselves – without needing you to step in and do it for them.

Discussing Written Feedback

Most learners are better speakers than writers. Speech is a natural function of the human body. Writing is a technology we have to learn. A cultural product which was invented many thousands of years ago and which has been passed down ever since.

We can use speech to quickly and efficiently refine, edit and compose our thoughts. Talking things through is a way to create meaning. We make sense of problems by talking about them. We get a better understanding of our own thinking by talking about it.

Discussion is a form of verbal rehearsal. When we discuss something, we rehearse our ideas about it. If we discuss something a few times, those ideas become more secure and more refined. We reach a better level of understanding by practising speaking our ideas out loud.

We can bring all these benefits to bear when learners are faced with written feedback by discussing it with them. The process of discussion scaffolds learners' interactions with the written feedback. It helps them to come to terms with it.

For example, we might be working with a small group of learners in a literacy lesson. We begin by giving them back their books, which we took in at the end of the last session. Each book contains written feedback we want learners to use in today's lesson. We invite the learners to read through their feedback and to then discuss it with a partner. We follow this up with a general discussion, in which we ask different learners to tell us about their feedback, which we then re-explain to them, further developing the discussion.

After five minutes of this, all learners in the group are well placed to apply their feedback in the next part of the lesson. The discussion has scaffolded their interaction with it, helping them to understand it and to make sense of it.

Highlighting

Consider this:

'Jake, I like the way you have included examples of how migration has affected different countries. This shows you understand the differences between different types of migration. I've highlighted these strengths in blue. I'd now like you to try explaining how governments might respond differently to different types of migration. I've highlighted in yellow where you could have included this thinking in your work. See if you can add it in now.'

Here, the teaching assistant has given their learner some feedback. They've then used two highlighter pens to indicate which parts of the work the feedback refers to. This scaffolds the feedback by making it easier for the learner to see what the feedback means, what it refers to and what the teaching assistant has been thinking about when they've given their feedback.

You can use this technique on a regular basis. If you do, stick to the same colours for strengths and targets. This way, your learners will quickly come to associate, say, blue with strengths and yellow with targets. This speeds up the process of recognition and assimilation of feedback.

Another option is to highlight student work in response to written feedback provided by the teacher. For example, imagine a teaching assistant is working one-to-one with a learner in a science lesson. The learner has a piece of work returned to them. At the end of this the teacher has provided a written comment. The learner is struggling to make sense of it, so the teaching assistant highlights the strengths referred to in the feedback with one colour, and the area for improvement with another colour. This makes it easier for the learner to work out what the comment means.

Model Reading Comprehension Strategies

Some learners are better at reading than others. But all learners can improve their reading. Written feedback needs to be read. If a learner struggles with their reading, they may be at a disadvantage when it comes to engaging with their feedback. We can help them overcome this by modelling reading comprehension strategies. This means showing learners different strategies they can use to unpick and decode a text they are reading.

For example, we might imagine a teaching assistant who reads aloud the written feedback a learner has received. Having done this, they then read it a second time, but this time more slowly. As they read, they verbalise some of the strategies the learner could use to make sense of the feedback. They might ask questions of the feedback, or they might make connections between what the feedback says and what they already know, or they might connect the feedback to different elements of the work the learner has produced. Each of these is an example of a reading comprehension strategy. These are the tools we use to help us understand what we are reading, as we read it.

Having modelled how to use a series of reading comprehension strategies to unpick a piece of written feedback, you can pass things over to your learner and ask them to have a go. It is better if you invite them to try using one comprehension strategy at a time. This stops the learner getting overloaded and gives them a chance to become familiar with the strategy in question before moving onto another one.

The whole process is about demonstrating to learners how they can make sense of written feedback. You provide a model they can then apply. With practice, learners will come to internalise the strategies you show them, making it easier for them to read and understand written feedback in the future.

Model Comparing the Feedback to the Work

When learners receive written feedback about their work, we want them to be able to make sense of that feedback in the context of what they have produced. This means they can look at their work and say 'OK, so that refers to that, the target is based on this,' and so on. We want them to understand that the teacher or the teaching assistant has looked at their work, assessed it and given them feedback in response to this. The feedback is based on the work. It refers to different parts of it.

You can help learners to engage with their feedback in this way by modelling the process for them. Here's what it might look like:

Teaching Assistant: 'OK, I'm going to pretend I wrote the essay. So, let me have a look at the feedback Mr Taylor has written and I'll see if I can connect it to different parts of the essay. Right, well this first strength is to do with the introduction. Let me go back and have a look…yeah, OK, so I can see that he is talking about this particular bit [teaching assistant points at the work]. Now, the next strength is a more general one, its about how I kept trying to answer the question in every paragraph. Right, let me have a look through and see if I can find this…yeah, that paragraph…that one as well…and that one [teaching assistant points at a series of paragraphs]. Last thing then, what about this target? It's to do with the conclusion. Let me re-read that…OK, yeah, I can see what sir's saying [teaching assistant points at the conclusion] it could be better, couldn't it? Shall we have a go at rewriting it?'

In this example, the teaching assistant carefully models how to compare a piece of written feedback with the work that feedback is about. The process gives meaning to the feedback and makes it easier for the learner to understand what has been said and why.

Summary

In this chapter we've examined some of the ways in which you can make written feedback more accessible for your learners. We've looked at scaffolding and modelling techniques you can use to help learners make sense of their feedback. The five techniques are:

1) Breaking down written feedback so learners can focus on one element at a time.

2) Discussing written feedback so learners can edit, refine and order their thoughts about what it means.

3) Using different colours to highlight strengths and areas for improvement so learners can quickly see what their feedback refers to.

4) Modelling reading comprehension strategies for learners to copy, imitate or borrow from

5) Modelling how to compare your work to your feedback.

Chapter 9 – Feedback Troubleshooting

Everything so far has been based on the idea that you can successfully deliver feedback to your learners and that they are happy to take it in board and use it. But what if things go wrong? Or what if you run into difficulties? In this chapter, we look at five of the most common issues which can arise when you give feedback. And we present solutions to help you overcome each one.

Your Learner Ignores Your Feedback

Some learners will ignore feedback. This could be for a variety of reasons. A learner might have a general dislike of feedback. They may not see the value of your feedback, or they may feel feedback has no point. They might ignore your feedback because they don't understand it or because they cannot see how it relates to them and their work. And some learners may ignore feedback because they believe they cannot change so what is the point in listening to someone telling you that you can.

If a learner ignores your feedback, it is better to talk to them about their actions rather than gloss over it. Glossing over risks normalising the behaviour. If you don't deal with it now, the learner may assume they can behave in that way in the future and so repeat the action again and again. But we know that feedback is important – that it is about teachers and teaching assistants giving access to their expertise to help learners progress and develop.

Begin by asking your learner how they felt about your feedback. Ask them what reaction they had to it and why they think they had this reaction. Then, ask what made them decide to ignore it. Make clear at this stage that you are not being judgemental – you simply want to ascertain the facts and get to the bottom of the situation.

Once the learner has shared their feelings and the reasoning behind their decision, you are in a much stronger position from which to talk to them about what has happened. They will also feel they have been given a voice. And it is much harder to argue against someone who is being calm, rational and polite, as you will be when following this process.

Finally, talk to your learner about why feedback matters. Explain that feedback is a tool any learner can use to improve their work. That it is something teachers and teaching assistants give to all learners and that it is a neutral act – neither positive nor negative. Indicate that feedback is information the learner can use to change things. That it gives access to expertise they would otherwise have trouble accessing. Talking in this way helps learners to see feedback in a more positive light.

Conclude matters by inviting the learner to have a go at implementing their feedback. Offer to help them in this and suggest you tackle the problem as a team, working together.

Your Learner Gets Defensive About Feedback

Some learners get defensive about feedback, perceiving it as a threat or an identification of what they lack. Sometimes this is because the learner is operating under a fixed mindset. Learners with a fixed mindset believe that intelligence, talent and ability are not open to change. They believe they have what they have, and that's the end of it. For learners who are thinking in this way, feedback can feel pointless, even threatening. It's as if someone is telling them what they can't do and leaving it at that – because the learner doesn't believe they can change, so how could the feedback help?

If a learner gets defensive about feedback, try not to react in a similar way. Often, learners can unwittingly transfer emotions onto us. For example, a teaching assistant might deliver some feedback to a learner, see that learner getting defensive and rejecting the feedback, and then respond in kind by getting defensive themselves.

This can easily happen, but rarely gives rise to good outcomes.

A better option is to take a step back and say something like: 'Oh, that's interesting. I was giving you feedback to try and help you get better, but you didn't see it in that way. Why do you think that was?' This approach douses any possibility of conflict and turns the situation into an investigation that you and the learner can conduct together.

After discussing the learner's response, you can go on to explain why feedback matters and what you think about the learner's potential for change and development. Say something like: 'When I give you feedback it's because I want to find ways to help you get better. I know that all learners can improve, whatever their starting points. You can use my feedback to develop your thinking and your work more quickly than would otherwise be the case. It's like a gift, from me to you.'

You Are Not Sure What Feedback to Give

On some occasions you will be unsure what feedback to give. You may not have a full understanding of where a learner is at, or you might feel there are various pieces of feedback you could give but are finding it tricky to choose between them. We'll look at each in turn.

If you don't have a full understanding of where a learner is at with their learning, and are struggling to give feedback as a result, remember that your key focus is eliciting information about their learning. You can elicit information in lots of different ways – by listening, observing, reading their work, talking to the learner, and asking them questions.

If you need to bring yourself swiftly up to speed, for example if you are asked to work with a learner you've not previously supported, then the best approach is to ask if you can have a quick read through their book. Follow this up with a discussion about what the learner knows and understands in which you ask most of the questions. This will help you to elicit useful information about where the learner is at. You are then in a much better position from which to give feedback.

If you have several different pieces of feedback you feel you could give but feel uncertain about which one to share with your learner, a slightly different approach suggests itself. First, ask yourself whether one of your pieces of feedback is more important than the others. If it is, go with that one. If, on the other hand, none stand out, ask yourself which piece of feedback the learner could make best use of now, in the moment. If one piece presents itself, share this with the learner. If one does not, remind yourself that it is better for learners to focus on one piece of feedback at a time. This compels you to make a choice and, in so doing, you will have a single piece of feedback ready to share, along with the knowledge that you can share the other pieces later.

You Don't Have Time to Give Feedback

If you don't have time to give feedback you need to make time. As we pointed out in the introduction, feedback has been shown to have a hugely positive impact on learner achievement. We should therefore prioritise giving feedback, putting it ahead of some of the other things we do in the classroom. With that said, if time is short, here are three techniques you can use to deliver feedback efficiently and effectively:

1) In advance of the lesson, make a note of which of your learners you want to give feedback to and what feedback you want to give. Take this into the lesson with you and

keep it close at hand. As the lesson progresses, remind yourself of the note and tick off each learner as you give them feedback. This helps to keep you on track and makes it easy for you to weave the delivery of feedback into what you are doing during the lesson.

2) If you are supporting a single learner throughout a lesson, begin that lesson by giving them feedback. This means thinking back to what the learner has been doing most recently and giving them feedback on this. You can then invite the learner to make use of your feedback during the lesson. The advantage of this method is that you deliver feedback right at the beginning of the lesson, meaning you don't forget to do it and you don't run out of time.

3) At the end of the lesson, take five minutes before you leave the classroom to note down some feedback in the books of the learners you've been working with. While this does take up an extra five minutes, it means you can give feedback while the lesson is still fresh in your mind and it also means that when learners return and take their books out again your feedback will be the first thing they see.

There is No Time for Learners to Implement Your Feedback

If learners don't have time in which to implement your feedback then that feedback may well disappear into the ether, never to be seen again. This isn't deliberate avoidance on the part of the learner, it's just that lessons move on quickly and it's easy to forget about feedback as your focus moves onto other things. Here are five techniques you can use to ensure there is time in which learners can implement your feedback:

1) Use the red box technique from Chapter Seven. This is where you draw a red box underneath the written feedback you have given. Learners must then have a go at implementing their feedback within the red box – meaning you and they can both see what the results of this are.

2) Link the feedback to the lesson. If your learner understands how your feedback links to the lesson, it becomes easier for them to implement that feedback during the lesson. This is about creating a connection in the learner's mind between your feedback and the work they are currently doing.

3) Give feedback at the start of the lesson. As per the previous entry. Giving feedback at the start of the lesson means giving learners the longest time possible to act on that feedback. You could give feedback on what learners did last time round, or feedback on their general efforts to date. Either way, your target will be something they can work towards in the rest of the lesson.

4) Review feedback halfway through the lesson. Halfway through the lesson, take two or three minutes out. Use this time to speak to your learners about their feedback. Ask them how they are finding it, whether they think they have successfully implemented it and what they might need to do next. This draws learners' attention back to their feedback and keeps it at the forefront of their minds.

5) Write feedback on a slip of paper and place this on the learner's desk. Doing this means the feedback is clearly available throughout the lesson, easy for the learner to see and easy for them to focus on.

Summary

In this chapter we've focussed on feedback troubleshooting. We've looked at various problems which might arise, related to feedback, and explored ways in which you can overcome these. The five problems to which we gave solutions are:

1) What to do if your learner ignores your feedback.

2) What to do if learners get defensive about feedback.

3) What to do if you are not sure about what feedback to give.

4) What to do if you don't have time to give feedback.

5) What to do if learners don't have time to implement your feedback.

Chapter 10 – Conclusion: Recapping and Next Steps

Feedback is a powerful tool. It is a way to give learners access to your expertise. You can use feedback to help learners change what they are doing, adapt, modify and develop their ideas, knowledge, understanding and skills. Feedback is about helping learners understand what they have done well and what they can improve. It can be written, verbal or a combination of the two. Feedback should be given with the intention of its being used by the learner. This may mean helping the learner to use your feedback. Or, it might mean setting aside specific time in which learners can focus on putting their feedback into practice.

If something is getting in the way of you delivering feedback – or getting in the way of your learners using your feedback – look for ways to overcome the issue. The importance of feedback is too great to let it be swept aside by the busyness of the classroom or the other matters making demands on learners' attention.

In this book we've looked at a whole host of strategies and techniques you can use to ensure your feedback is of the highest standard. Let's recap these here, bringing them together in one place for ease of reference:

Chapter 2

Good feedback tends to follow these rules:

1) It is personalised. The learner knows it is for them and feels that it addresses their current situation.

2) It is precise and relevant. The learner can see how the feedback connects to what they are doing.

3) It combines positives and negatives. The learner receives information about what they are doing well and what they can do to improve.

4) It is clear. The learner can understand it and use it.

5) It is concise. The learner is not overloaded by the feedback. They can use it to target their efforts.

Chapter 3

When giving verbal feedback, there are lots of options open to us. We should aim to follow the rules for good feedback outlined in Chapter Two. As well as this, we can think about specific strategies through which to shape our feedback. These include:

1) Critically observing what learners are doing, then giving feedback.

2) Critically observing what learners are doing, giving feedback in response, then leaving and returning a little later to see how learners have used the feedback.

3) Providing feedback in the form of a question – or a series of questions.

4) Suggesting alternatives and then discussing these with our learners.

5) Drawing attention to learners' strengths, so as to reinforce these.

Chapter 4

In Chapter Four we examined a further five techniques you can use to structure your verbal feedback. These are:

1) Providing two options from which the learner can select.

2) Linking your feedback to positive changes in the future.

3) Giving feedback on misconceptions.

4) Creating a feedback crib sheet to help you out during lessons.

5) Inviting learners to tell you the area or areas on which they would like feedback.

Chapter 5

In Chapter Five we looked at scaffolding and modelling verbal feedback. This is where we help learners to access our feedback. The five techniques we explored are:

1) Breaking feedback down so it is easier for learners to understand.

2) Asking learners if they can explain your feedback back to you – and making changes in response to this.

3) Specifying what success looks like so learners know what they are aiming for.

4) Demonstrating how to use your feedback.

5) Drawing out a plan of action learners can use to direct their efforts.

Chapter 6

In starting to think about written feedback we explored some of its key characteristics and features. We thought about these in the context of learning and looked at the impact written feedback might have on our learners. Five things to think about, use and employ when working with learners are:

1) Remember that written feedback fixes information in time and space. This brings many benefits we and our learners can take advantage of.

2) The best time to give written feedback is when you know learners will have a chance to think about it, reflect on it and use it after they've received it.

3) You can track written feedback – something you can't do with verbal feedback.

4) There are a range of strategies you can employ to help learners feel in control of their written feedback.

5) Combining written and verbal feedback can have a good impact on student learning.

Chapter 7

In Chapter Seven we further explored written feedback, looking at a variety of techniques you can use to structure it and to help learners access, understand and engage with the written feedback they receive. The five techniques we looked at are:

1) Giving three strengths followed by a target, to help learners feel positive about constructive criticism.

2) Giving two stars and wish, achieving the same result, but in a slightly different way.

3) Drawing a red box underneath your feedback and inviting learners to show within that box how they could implement their feedback.

4) Giving examples to illustrate how learners can put your written targets into practice.

5) Supplementing written feedback with verbal explanation so it is easier for learners to make sense of the former.

Chapter 8

In Chapter Eight we examined some of the ways in which you can make written feedback more accessible for your learners. We looked at scaffolding and modelling techniques you can use to help learners make sense of their feedback. The five techniques are:

1) Breaking down written feedback so learners can focus on one element at a time.

2) Discussing written feedback so learners can edit, refine and order their thoughts about what it means.

3) Highlighting strengths and areas for improvement in different colours so learners can quickly see what their feedback refers to.

4) Modelling reading comprehension strategies for learners to copy, imitate or borrow from.

5) Modelling how to compare your work to your feedback.

Chapter 9

In Chapter Nine we focussed on feedback troubleshooting. We looked at various problems which might arise, related to feedback, and explored ways in which you can overcome these. The five problems to which we gave solutions are:

1) What to do if your learner ignores your feedback.

2) What to do if learners get defensive about feedback.

3) What to do if you are not sure about what feedback to give.

4) What to do if you don't have time to give feedback.

5) What to do if learners don't have time to implement your feedback.

And with that, we draw the book to a close. By following the rules from Chapter Two and using the strategies and techniques outlined in Chapters Three to Nine, you will be well placed to raise achievement, support your learners and help them to grow, learn and develop. Remember that feedback has been shown time and again to be a really effective tool through which to raise achievement. It gives learners access to your expertise and helps them to understand what they have done well and what they can do to improve things in the future. Feedback is a crucial part of what happens in the classroom. It is a crucial feature of the interactions you have with your learners. Giving good feedback, and doing so on a regular basis, can help you to have the best impact possible on your learners. Good luck in your efforts!

Select Bibliography

Anderson, Lorin W.; Krathwohl, David R., (eds), *A taxonomy for learning, teaching, and assessing: A revision of Bloom's taxonomy of educational objectives*. Harlow: Pearson Education, 2014

Black, Paul; Wiliam, Dylan, et al, *Assessment for Learning: Putting it into Practice.* Maidenhead: Open University Press, 2003

Black, Paul; Wiliam, Dylan, et al, *Working Inside the Black Box.* London: Letts, 1990

Bloom, B. S.; Engelhart, M. D.; Furst, E. J.; Hill, W. H.; Krathwohl, D. R., *Taxonomy of educational objectives: The classification of educational goals. Handbook I: Cognitive domain*. New York: David McKay Company, 1956

Hattie, John, *Visible Learning.* Abingdon: Routledge, 2009

Stobart, Gordon, *The Expert Learner.* Maidenhead: Open University Press, 2014

Wiliam, Dylan, *Assessment for learning: Why, what and how?* London: Institute of Education, 2009

Wiliam, Dylan, *Embedded Formative Assessment.* Bloomington: Solution Tree Press, 2011

Wiliam, Dylan; Black, Paul, *Inside the Black Box.* London: GL Assessment, 1990

Printed in Great Britain
by Amazon